£20.00

1951

D1391138

ISLAMIC
FRONTIERS OF
CHINA
SILK ROAD IMAGES

SCORPION PUBLISHING LTD, LONDON

©photographs: How Man Wong
©text: How Man Wong, Adel Awni Dajani and the Chinese Islamic
Cultural Association, London.

All rights reserved. No part of this publication may be reproduced,
stored in a retrieval system, or transmitted in any form or by any means,
electronic, mechanical, photocopying, recording or otherwise, without
the prior permission of the copyright owner.

First published in 1990 by Scorpion Publishing Ltd, Victoria House,
Buckhurst Hill, Essex, England.

ISBN 0 905906 83 7

General Editor: Leonard Harrow
Designer: Colin Larkin
Typeset in Linotype Berkeley Oldstyle Book 11½ point
Printed on 150gsm fineblade smooth
Printed and bound in England by Jolly and Barber, Rugby.

NOTE ON SPELLING OF PROPER NAMES
Every effort has been made to use modern and recognisable spellings for
Chinese and Muslim names. We seek the reader's indulgence for any
confusion in this respect.

1 *A solitary camel silhouetted against the foothills of the 7,546 metre
Mt. Muztagata (Father of Snow Mountains), a key passageway of the old
Silk Road through the Chinese Pamirs.*

ISLAMIC
FRONTIERS OF
CHINA
SILK ROAD IMAGES

photography and text HOW MAN WONG

co-author ADEL A DAJANI

ACKNOWLEDGEMENTS

A project of this nature is born by being kindled with the spark of an idea but then in order to survive has to be nurtured by the dedication of a great many people. HE Sheikh Duaij Jaber Al Ali Al Sabah and Sheikha Altaf Al Sabah were among the first to share our enthusiasm for the project and whose support helped to make the book a reality.

The government agencies and officials in China offered invaluable advice and assistance, in particular ex-Governor Huang Jingpo of Qinghai Province, Wu Tianfu, Liaison and Deputy Secretary General of Canton, Xe Liangying, ex-Director of Foreign Affairs Bureau of Xinjiang, the Islamic Association in Beijing, Canton, Ningxia and Xinjiang, and the Overseas Chinese Bureau of Qinghai, Gansu, Ningxia and Xinjiang were all responsible for co-ordinating and planning a logistically complicated and ambitious itinerary in China which involved covering over 20,000 kilometres by road.

We would like to thank the National Geographic Society whose long years of involvement with How Man's work included support of this expedition and Deborah Chan who first introduced us in Hong Kong and whose assistance during our field trips was most appreciated.

There were innumerable families and individuals who were extremely hospitable and helpful to our work during the time we were in China. Many of them were of Tajik, Sala, Kirgiz, Kazak, Uighur and Hui Islamic nationalities. To them we extend our most sincere gratitude and thanks. In particular Shams El Din of Xining, who gave us as a token of our visit one of the most precious possessions in his household and whose only request in exchange was not to forget the Muslims in China.

Finally we would like to thank our families without whose enthusiasm and support this project would have remained an unfulfilled dream.

How Man Wong   Adel Awni Dajani

PREFACE

'Seek knowledge, even if it may lie in China,' is a saying, or Hadith, commonly attributed to the Prophet Muhammad. This book traces the journey of two individuals who took the Prophet's words literally. Their paths ordinarily should have never crossed: How Man Wong, a Chinese from Los Angeles, who had dedicated his life to exploring China's frontier regions and who had become a recognised photo journalist; and Adel Dajani, a Palestinian Muslim, who whilst a law student in the UK became aware of the existence of the Chinese Muslims on his first trip to China in 1974.

They met through a mutual acquaintance in Hong Kong, which was How Man's habitual stopover on his way to China, and where Adel was working as a merchant banker. There the common chord was struck and in the summer of 1984 they began an expedition to seek the 'Islamic Frontier of China'.

The authors hope that through the pages of this book their readers will acquire a rare glimpse of a fascinating but relatively unknown region of Central Asia, a region where despite periods of isolation, Islam has adapted itself and survived for over 1,000 years. There is so much more 'knowledge to be sought' about the Chinese Muslims and if this book serves to stimulate that interest, it will have served its purpose.

There are about one billion Chinese in China. There are another billion Muslims in the rest of the world. A small bridge connects these two billion people which make up almost half of the world's population. The authors believe they have crossed that bridge – at the Islamic Frontier of China.

How Man Wong   Adel Awni Dajani
1989

2   *Imam Yang Sen is a noted Islamic scholar. He now teaches at the new mosque by the Yellow River in Lanzhou, Gansu Province.*

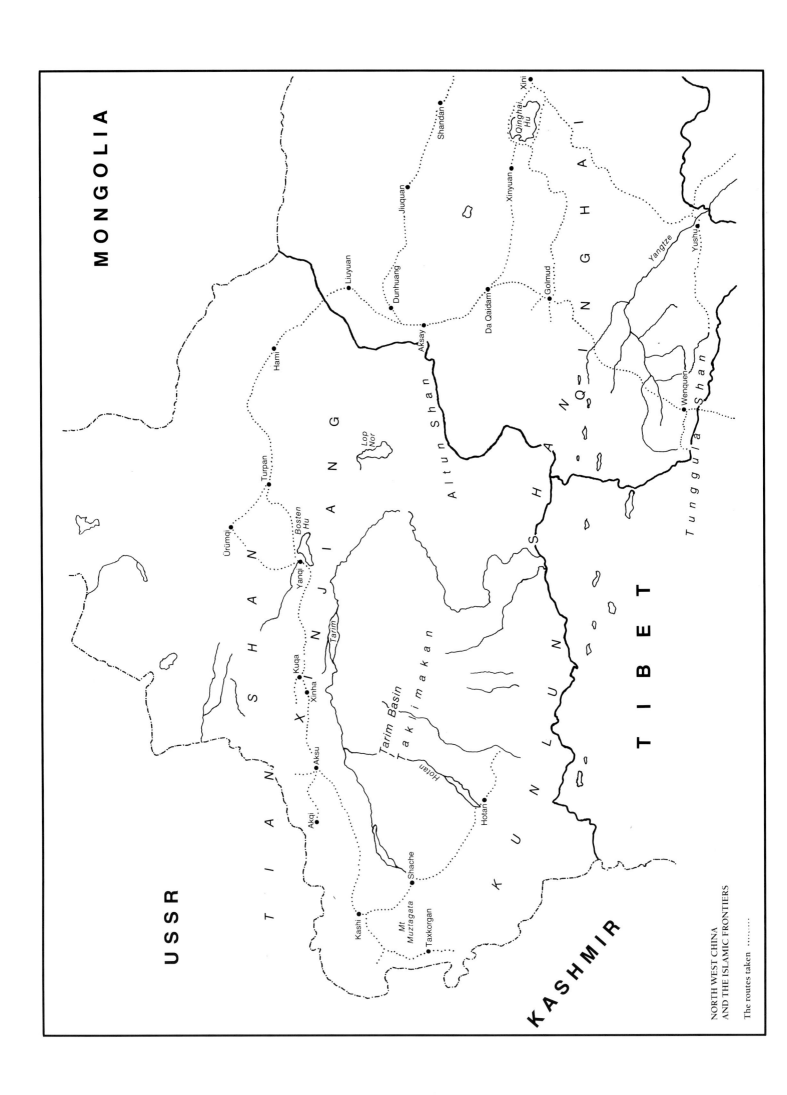

MONGOLIA

USSR

Shandan

Xini

Qinghai
Hu

Jiuquan

Xinyuan

Liuyuan

Dunhuang

Da Qaidam

Golmud

Q
I
N
G
H
A
I

Hami

Aksay

Altun Shan

Yangtze

Yushu

Lop
Nor

Turpan

K
U
N
L
U
N

S H A N

Wenquen

Tunggula Shan

Ürümqi

Bosten
Hu

T
I
B
E
T

Yanqi

S
H
A
N

Tarim

Kuqa

Xinha

Takllimakan

Hotan

T
I
A
N

X
I
N
J
I
A
N
G

Tarim Basin

Aksu

Akqi

Hotan

Hotan

K
U
N
L
U
N

Shache

Kashi

Mt
Muztagata

Taxkorgan

KASHMIR

NORTH WEST CHINA
AND THE ISLAMIC FRONTIERS

The routes taken ....

CONTENTS

PART 1

ANCIENT TRADE ROUTES

As the long train of the camel caravan leaves the Jade Gate and Sun Gate of western China, it enters the huge expanse of desert sands of the Gobi and Taklimakan, two of the largest deserts of Central Asia, and of the world.

Indeed, the famous Tang poet, Wang Wei, wrote: 'Gentlemen, be advised and drink another glass of wine, west of the Sun Gate you'll find no acquaintance.' To discourage the Chinese traveller even further, another Tang poet, Wang Ziwuen, lamented: 'Don't use the Qiang flute to complain about the willow, beyond the Jade Gate the wind of spring will not blow.'

However, neither cautionary poems nor the intimidating name 'Taklimakan', meaning 'going in without coming out', succeeded in daunting the most determined of travellers. Despite the extreme conditions of the journey and an inhospitable climate for settlers, a culture gradually developed along fringes of the deserts and their oases. Originating as waystations serving the ancient trade route between China and Central Asia, and later the Middle East and Europe, this fragile string of initial settlements in time flourished to become major trading posts and cultural centres of Central Asia. Names like Kumul (Hami), Piqan (Shanshan), Yutian (Hotan), Kashgar (Kashi) and Qongling (Taxkorgan) describe important places, synonymous with the old Silk Road.

There is no means of tracing precisely when the trade route was first used. However, historical records reveal that in the time of Julius Caesar, Romans were already intrigued by the fine quality of the silk from China. Silk continued to be one of the major commodities of this trade route until people of the Middle East and Europe learned the skills of sericulture. A story retold by the Tang pilgrim monk, Xuanzang, describes how a Chinese princess, on her way to marry a king in the west, took the well-guarded secret by hiding some silkworm eggs inside her hat and later taught her subjects to raise silkworms.

Many other items travelled the 'Silk Road'. From China, lacquer, porcelain, pepper, cassia, cinnibar, tea, spice, gold and silver ornaments, dye, musk and herbs were carried westward. Besides commodities and merchandise, there was the transfer of culture and technology. Paper making, gunpowder, the compass and the growing of cotton were also introduced to the West. In return China received from the West pearls, diamonds, gem stones, jade, glassware, ivory, camphor, amber, sandalwood, coral, sesame, herbs, horses and, at times, other exotic animals.

At different times over the centuries, some of these items became much sought-after commodities and small quantities of such items commanded huge prices. Other items seem to have been transported in such enormous quantities that they appear out of all proportion within the general volume of trade. For example, rhubarb from China was considered by people from the Middle East and Europe to be such a potent drug for all ailments, that huge amounts were exported. It was recorded in a Ming Dynasty account of the 14th century that in one month alone, of the 600 camels arriving at Samarkand, 300 were carrying rhubarb – or the equivalent of 100 tons. The people in the Middle East and Europe grew so accustomed to it that by the mid-1700s, the Qing Emperor, Qianlong, banned the export of rhubarb as a punitive measure because of unrest along China's western frontier.

With the development of trade on this western frontier, more and more traffic went between China and western states. As early as the Western Han Dynasty, the Emperor Wudi dispatched Zhang Qian as his emissary to Central Asia in the year 138 BC. Zhang returned to the capital after thirteen years with a tale which fascinated the emperor and his court. He went back for a second trip to the West and instigated an exchange of envoys between many Western kingdoms and the Han court.

3 (opposite) A Kazak woman in a traditionally embroidered veil which covers her head and neck. Now living in Aksay, western Gansu, her tribe was originally from the Altai region in northern Xinjiang, bordering the Soviet Union. Their mass migration took place in the 1930s as they evaded the oppressive rule of the warlords. Today the Kazak in China total slightly over one million.

4 (following pages) A Tajik bride wears a red scarf and has her hair braided and decorated with strings of buttons. Needlework with colourful geometric designs adorns the traditional hats of the women. The Tajiks have Middle Eastern features and speak Persian.

5 (following pages) The wife of Ahung (Imam) Ma Deming of Yangjiaxiang mosque in Xining. Old Hui women wear a partial veil in black, while the middle aged women wear white and the young ones green.

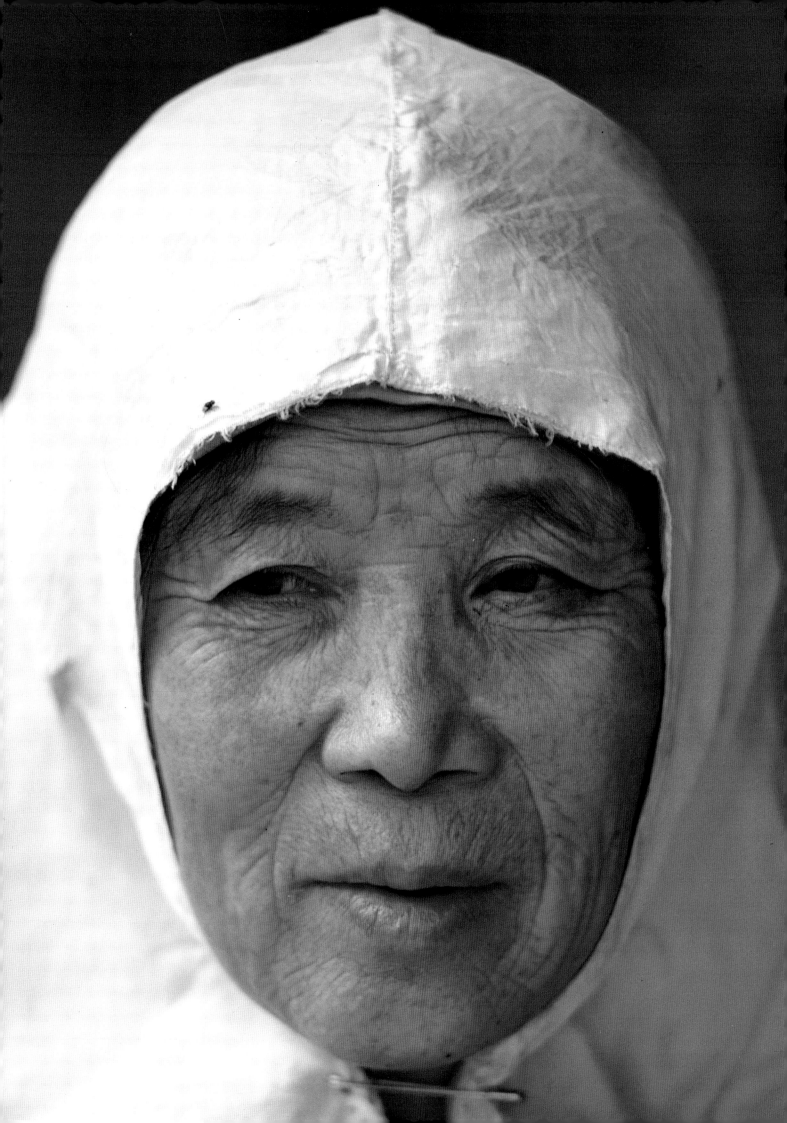

6 (previous pages) A Kazak man of Aksay in western Gansu Province sporting a white cap with little flower designs.

7 (previous pages) A woman of the Hui minority wears a veil covering part of her head.

9 (opposite) A Hui man in a park next to the Yellow River at Lanzhou, provincial capital of Gansu. The quartz glasses are popular among older Hui men and real quartz ones are usually very expensive.

10 (following pages) Minarets and the domed roof of a mosque silhouetted against an approaching storm at Lanzhou by the Yellow River.

11 (following pages) Imam Yang Sen teaches Arabic to students after their regular school hours at the new mosque on the bank of the river at Lanzhou.

12 (following pages) A Hui sculptor applies his skills to the outside wall of Yinchuan's big mosque of Ningxia, Hui Autonomous Region in northern China.

13 (following pages) An older Hui calligrapher of Yinchuan adopts the traditional Chinese brush and ink in writing the Arabic script.

8 A Tajik woman in the Chinese Pamirs.

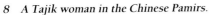

14   A Hui woman at Xining displays a glass frame of Mecca, painted in gold and white.

15   A Hui ahung (imam) *studies in his home at Chengzhou in central China, seated on a kang. This is a cement bed usually connected to the kitchen and is effectively heated by the hearth during the cold winter months.*

Many 'embassies' to the Chinese capitals were in reality made up of merchants who thereby enjoyed the benefits conferred by official status. Adopting the name 'envoy', or calling a journey a 'tribute', the 'envoy' would enjoy favourable treatment along the way. His party would be entertained by local officials en route, his merchandise would not be taxed and it would be guarded through insecure regions. At the end of the journey, perhaps in Changan, he would be handsomely rewarded by the emperor. After all, the Son of Heaven had to bestow on the 'envoy' fine gifts to display his wealth and graciousness. Consequently there was no shortage of envoys on the road and their paths frequently crossed.

Such constant trade gives a misleading impression. The road was not a highway to peace and prosperity: the journey was extremely dangerous. The Tang pilgrim monk, Xuanzang, describes in his travels how he found his way by following the remains of human and animal bones. There was the constant threat of bandits. Grottoes numbers 45 and 420 of the Sui (589-618 AD) and Tang (618-907 AD) dynasties, at Dunhuang near the Jade Gate, have murals depicting the danger of travelling and bandits waylaying a caravan. Along the Silk Road many Buddhist grottoes and shrines were constructed where prayers could be made to ensure a safe journey or the gods could be thanked upon a safe return.

16   *A Hui ahung reads the Koran in Arabic at a mosque in Kaifeng in Hunan.*

17   (opposite) At the mosque outside Turfan, an Uygur arrives for early morning Friday prayer.

18   Inside the mosque at Turfan, Uygurs congregate for prayers under the traditional structure.

19   (following pages) At the great mosque of Xining over 5,000 Muslims converge every Friday for prayer. As the main building is filled, people overflow into the huge courtyard.

It was also during the reign of Wudi in the Western Han Dynasty (206 BC-9 AD) that military conquest in the western region took on a more significant role. In an obsessive quest to acquire the legendary horses of Central Asia, an army of 60,000 men was sent forth. After an arduous journey with considerable losses, they reached Dahuan, where only 30,000 soldiers remained to besiege the city. However, the attack was successful and the kingdom of Dahuan surrendered. The best steeds were offered as tribute to the far-away Han Emperor.

It is to be noted that as a result of military conquests, skills and technology as well as booty and prisoners were acquired by the victors. For example, after the Battle of Talas (a city in today's Soviet Central Asia) between China and Tashin (Arabs) in the mid-8th century, papermaking was introduced to Central Asia by Chinese prisoners of war. Later, during the conquests of the Mongol Yuan Dynasty in the 13th century, scientists and technicians were brought back from the Middle East to China. The architectural layout of Beijing, then capital of the Mongols, was based on the design of a Muslim architect, Ikhtiyar al-Din.

20   *At the Yangjiaxiang mosque of Xining, Ahung Ma Deming leads prayers in Arabic.*

Although caravans travelled from the Chinese capital to Central Asia, few travellers, if any, went all the way to Europe or vice versa. Chinese merchandise appearing in the West and in the market in Rome arrived through a relay of trade rather than a single marathon journey. Rarely is a European found in the Chinese capital prior to the Ming Dynasty. Marco Polo, who came to China from Venice and stayed for seventeen years during the Yuan Dynasty, was a latter-day exception. That is why his account of a fascinating land became so intriguing to people in the West.

22 (following pages) A Chinese version of the minbar from which the ahung or imam would deliver his sermon.

23 (following pages) At the Canton mosque a Hui youth practises a specialised form of the martial arts, developed by the Muslims to defend themselves.

21 At Tongxin in the Ningxia Hui Autonomous Region, an old mosque was once used to house the Communist People's Army during its famed Long March between 1934 and 1935.

In the trading process, the people of Central Asia had always served as middlemen between two continents. There were times when the Chinese made an effort to explore direct trade routes to Europe. Each time they were turned back by the stories of their trading partners in the Middle East. A work from 430 AD relates how an emissary led by Gaying was sent from the Eastern Han court. He got as far as Persia and was told by a local boatman that three years' provisions were needed to sail beyond. This, coupled with stories of impending danger, caused him to turn back. Previously, in 166 AD, an envoy from Syria had been sent to China by the Roman Empire during the rule of Marcus Aurelius Antonius, also seeking direct trade contact with the Chinese.

At the height of Chinese dynastic rule during the Tang period, and at a time when the Silk Road in western China was becoming a thoroughfare for merchants, pilgrims and diplomatic envoys, another trade route was developing in the south along the China coast. Aided by the seafaring knowledge and navigational skills of the Arabs, ships were docking at the coastal cities of Canton, Yangzhou, Hangzhou and Quanzhou.

It is recorded that the monk Fa Xian left Changan in 399 AD and travelled to India by land. After fifteeen years of journeying and staying in the Indian sub-continent, he set off for Canton by the sea route. The monsoon took his boat with over 200 people way off course to Java but he later boarded another boat from Java destined for Canton. Though the unfortunate monk again ran into a storm and ended up in Qingtao to the north, it demonstrates that as early as the 4th century, the sea route to China was, despite its danger, quite a regular service.

Under the Tang Dynasty, the city of Changan (present-day Xian) at the eastern end of the Silk Road and Khamfu (today's Canton) on the South China Sea each housed tens of thousands of foreigners, predominantly Arabs from the Middle East. It is recorded that during that time there were over 10,000 foreign households in Changan, then capital of China, and the Imperial College had over 8,000 foreign students enrolled. The famous Tang poet, Li Po, described many hostels and restaurants operated by people with Middle Eastern ancestry. In the south, the Huang Cha'ao uprising of 879 AD in Canton decimated 120,000 foreign residents. Whilst accounts of the massacre referred to the dead as 'Mohammedans, Christians, Jews and Parsee,' it is believed that the majority of them were Muslims.

Throughout Chinese history and with the rise and fall of dynasties, that part of the population with non-Han ancestry likewise fluctuated in influence, gained and lost favour, but it always remained an important part of the nation. Many of these people had settled in China, intermarried with Han Chinese and had, over the generations, became fully-fledged Chinese citizens. Today they are one of China's largest minority groups, the Hui.

Along China's inner Asian frontier, there are today many other ethnic groups who are Muslims. They are the Uygur, Kazak, Kirgiz, Sala, Tajik, Uzbek, Tartar, Dongxiang and Baoan. Each of these groups either originated within the present boundaries of China, or settled there over the centuries. They embody a history, culture and lifestyle quite different from the Han majority. Together, these nine groups, and the seven and a half million Hui, have an official population of over 15 million out of China's billion people; the Uygur 6 million, the Kazak 1.1 million, the Dongxiang 300,000, the Kirgiz 120,000, the Sala 70,000, the Tajik 28,000, the Uzbek 13,000, the Baoan 10,000 and the Tartar 5,000. Different as they are, there is one cohesive bond that binds them together – Islam.

24 (opposite) Muslims congregate at the mosque of Canton, claimed by many Chinese Muslims to be the oldest mosque in the country dating back to the 7th century.

25 (following pages) The landscape and palm trees of Hainan Island in the South China Sea is home to two Muslim villages, whose founders arrived by the sea route from southeast Asia.

26 (previous pages) At a mosque along the southern shore of Hainan Island, the local ahung, or imam, addresses devotees. The villagers of Yanglan claim that their ancestors came by way of the sea route from the Middle East.

27 (right) At the mausoleum housing the tomb of the king of Hami, his queen and relatives, an old attendant stands guard.

28 (bottom) While the tiled structure of the Hami king's mausoleum with its domed roof shows a strong Middle Eastern architectural influence, an adjacent building with curved eaves is unmistakably Chinese in style.

29 (opposite top) Arabic epigraphy graces the mosque of Tongxin in the Ningxia Hui Autonomous Region. Chinese wooden brackets support the overhanging eaves.

30 (opposite bottom) Arabic inscriptions and designs of Middle Eastern inspiration adorn the majestic arched doorway of the mosque at Kuqa in western Xinjiang.

31 (previous pages) Standing high on two front corners of the tomb of Appak Hoja at Kashgar on the Silk Road, these minaret-like towers, built around 1873, are decorated with glazed ceramic tiles and reliefs.

32 (previous pages) The mosque outside Turfan has a memorial minaret built around 1799 and dedicated to King Imin. It incorporates some of the most decorative designs in brick architecture in western China.

33 (top) The great mosque at Yinchuan with its five domed roofs bears a strong resemblance to the architecture of the Islamic homeland.

34 (bottom) At a roadside mosque at Kuqa, two towers stand as the minarets common to many mosques. Smaller mosques like this help bind the local community together.

35 (opposite top) Floral and geometric designs adorn the ceiling of the entrance to a mosque outside Kashgar.

36 (opposite bottom) Murals of flowers and vases surround a creative use of Arabic script decorating the walls of an old village mosque of the Salar people at Xunhua in Qinghai Province.

فَلَا أُقْسِمُ بِالْخُنَّسِ الْجَوَارِ الْكُنَّسِ وَالَّيْلِ إِذَا عَسْعَسَ ۝

وَالصُّبْحِ إِذَا تَنَفَّسَ ۝ إِنَّهُ لَقَوْلُ رَسُولٍ كَرِيمٍ ذِي قُوَّةٍ ۝

عِنْدَ ذِي الْعَرْشِ مَكِينٍ مُطَاعٍ ثَمَّ أَمِينٍ ۝ وَمَا صَاحِبُكُم

بِمَجْنُونٍ ۝ وَلَقَدْ رَآهُ بِالْأُفُقِ الْمُبِينِ ۝ وَمَا هُوَ عَلَى

الْغَيْبِ بِضَنِينٍ ۝ وَمَا هُوَ بِقَوْلِ شَيْطَانٍ رَجِيمٍ ۝ فَأَيْنَ

تَذْهَبُونَ ۝ إِنْ هُوَ إِلَّا ذِكْرٌ لِلْعَالَمِينَ ۝ لِمَن شَاءَ مِنكُمْ أَن

يَسْتَقِيمَ ۝ وَمَا تَشَاؤُونَ إِلَّا أَن يَشَاءَ اللَّهُ رَبُّ الْعَالَمِينَ ۝

سورة التطفيف مكية وهي ستّ وثلاثون آية

بِسْمِ اللَّهِ الرَّحْمَٰنِ الرَّحِيمِ

إِذَا السَّمَاءُ انْفَطَرَتْ ۝ وَإِذَا الْكَوَاكِبُ انْتَثَرَتْ ۝ وَإِذَا

الْبِحَارُ فُجِّرَتْ ۝ وَإِذَا الْقُبُورُ بُعْثِرَتْ ۝ عَلِمَتْ نَفْسٌ مَا

وَأَبِيهِ وَصَاحِبَتِهِ وَبَنِيهِ لِكُلِّ امْرِئٍ مِنْهُمْ يَوْمَئِذٍ

شَأْنٌ يُغْنِيهِ وُجُوهٌ يَوْمَئِذٍ مُسْفِرَةٌ ضَاحِكَةٌ مُسْتَبْشِرَةٌ

وَوُجُوهٌ يَوْمَئِذٍ عَلَيْهَا غَبَرَةٌ تَرْهَقُهَا قَتَرَةٌ أُولَئِكَ

هُمُ الْكَفَرَةُ الْفَجَرَةُ

بِسْمِ اللَّهِ الرَّحْمَنِ الرَّحِيمِ

إِذَا الشَّمْسُ كُوِّرَتْ وَإِذَا النُّجُومُ انْكَدَرَتْ وَإِذَا

الْجِبَالُ سُيِّرَتْ وَإِذَا الْعِشَارُ عُطِّلَتْ وَإِذَا الْوُحُوشُ

حُشِرَتْ وَإِذَا الْبِحَارُ سُجِّرَتْ وَإِذَا النُّفُوسُ زُوِّجَتْ

وَإِذَا الْمَوْءُودَةُ سُئِلَتْ بِأَيِّ ذَنْبٍ قُتِلَتْ وَإِذَا الصُّحُفُ

نُشِرَتْ وَإِذَا السَّمَاءُ كُشِطَتْ وَإِذَا الْجَحِيمُ

سُعِّرَتْ وَإِذَا الْجَنَّةُ أُزْلِفَتْ عَلِمَتْ نَفْسٌ مَا أَحْضَرَتْ

ISLAM COMES TO CHINA

In all the provinces, there is a town for the Moslems and in this they reside. They also have cells, colleges and mosques and are made much by the Emperor. In a certain part of this province is a town in which Moslems reside. It has a market and a mosque and a cell for the poor. Here is also a judge and a Sheikh al Islam; nor is there any doubt that there must be in all the towns Moslem merchants who have a judge and a Sheikh ul Islam to whom matters are referred.

The country referred to in the quotation is China, the date 1324-1325 AD and the writer, the famous Arab traveller Ibn Battuta, who had left his native Tangiers and travelled extensively throughout Asia and China, a little more than thirty years after Marco Polo had left the Far East.

Ibn Battuta was, from a historical perspective, a relative latecomer to China since commercial exchange between China and the Middle East dates back to pre-Islamic times, justifying the historical epitaph of the 'Arabs as the carriers of the world between the East and West'. The overland route, the Silk Road, was the world's longest trade route and reached from China to Constantinople and onto Rome, and the hazardous sea route stretched from Siraf in the Arab Gulf, through the Straits of Malacca and on to Canton. These two most vital arteries of trade formed the natural channels of commercial, cultural and, at a later stage, religious contact between the Arab world and China.

However, the official entry of Islam into China is obscured by romantic legends and folklore and is difficult to verify, since Islam was not carried to China as part of a proselytizing mission but flowed naturally along well-defined trade arteries between China and the Middle East. A legend amongst the Chinese Muslims links the coming of Islam to China with the Emperor T'ai Tsung, the second ruler of the Tang Dynasty and one of China's greatest emperors, who laid the framework of governmental institutions that were to last for the next millennium.

37 (previous pages) Two pages from an ancient Koran, purportedly carried by Salar ancestors when they migrated from Samarkand some 700 years ago. Today the book is a sacred relic of the Salar people in Qinghai Province.

38 (previous pages) Along the southern stretches of the Silk Road in Hotan, women in remote villages still boil the silkworm cocoon in time-honoured fashion and reel the silk with hand-cranked wooden wheels. The black and white dress of the woman is a traditional pattern made from silk.

39 (previous pages) A woman of Hotan spinning silk with a traditional wooden machine as her child watches.

40 (previous pages) In the countryside of Hotan on the southern Silk Road, Uygur weavers work a loom as they make a wool carpet with traditional designs.

41 (previous pages) An old Uygur man displays a silk carpet in traditional design that he wove as a child with his father decades ago. Resilient and durable, some of the more decorative silk carpets are hung on walls rather than used on the floor.

42 (previous pages) An old man in a village near Hotan weaves silk into fabric as he works on a wooden loom similar to those used many centuries ago.

44 (following pages) Sunday markets and bazaars along the Silk Road are the most popular sites for business transactions. Thousands attend the one at Kuqa by the river banks, while the bazaar at Kashgar has tens of thousands in attendance. Mule and horse carts bring all kinds of goods to be sold or exchanged.

43 A morning sun shines through poplar and willow trees in Hami, silhouetting a man preparing his mule cart for work.

T'ai Tsung came to the throne in 626, four years after the Prophet Muhammad and his followers left Mecca for Medina. The foundations for two movements that would change the course of history were being established in the far-flung towns of Medina and Sian, the capital of the Tang Dynasty. According to Chinese Muslim legend, one night T'ai Tsung had a dream:

> I dreamed of a turbaned man and of monsters . . . The man in the turban, with his hands clasped and murmuring prayers, pursued the monsters . . . To look on, he (had) indeed a strange countenance, totally unlike ordinary men; his face was the colour of black gold . . . his moustache and beard were cut . . . short and even; he had phoenix eyebrows, and a high nose and black eyes. His clothes were white and powdered, a jewelled girdle of jade encircled his loins, on his head was . . . a cloth turban like a coiled dragon. His presence was awe-inspiring. . .

When he entered he knelt towards the West, reading the book he held in his hand. When the monsters saw him they were at once changed into . . . proper forms, and in distressful voices pleaded for forgiveness. But the turbaned man read on for a little, till the monsters turned to blood and at last to dust, and at the sound of a voice the turbaned man disappeared.

45   In Kashgar, a sumptuous family banquet is given in honour of a little boy of seven to celebrate his circumcision and entry into manhood.

'Now,' continued the Emperor, 'I would like to know whether this be a good or an ill omen.' Thereupon the Interpreter of Dreams stepped out of the ranks of officials and said: 'The turbaned man is a Muslim from the West. Far beyond, in Arabia is a Muslim king of lofty mind and great virtue, whose country is wealthy and his troops are brave, and whose land produces rare and precious things, The customs of the country are liberal to a degree. I have heard that in the West a great Sage is born. On the natal day the sun showed many colours, the night was lengthened to eight watches, white clouds covered the hill tops, and when the True Book came from heaven a white vapour rose to the sky; therefore, because of the birth of the Sage favourable omens abounded. That the monsters entered the Palace indicates that strange and evil influences are at work in the heart of things, therefore came this omen of trouble. These monsters then must be dealt with by the Muslims if they are to be destroyed.' At that, a Prince of the Court named Han Shih-Ki stepped forward and said: 'I have heard well of the Muslims as being straight forward and true, gracious in their behaviour and loyal in their allegiance first and last. As to a plan for the present, throw open the pass, let communication be unhindered, place no restriction on intercourse and thus encourage peace. I beseech my lord to issue a decree sending an ambassador across the Western frontier to the Muslim king, asking him to send a sage to deal with the evils that threaten so that the country may be at peace.'

Hui-Hui Yuan-lai, as translated by C F Hogg-Marshall Broomhall, *Islam and China*

46 *A Hui man in Lanzou toasting bread on a metal burner. Besides selling his bread, he would also charge a small fee for people who bring their own flour dough.*

The legend continues that the Emperor dispatched an officer named Shih T'ang who went to Arabia and returned with three emissaries from the Prophet, one of whom was meant to be a companion of the Prophet and his maternal uncle, Sa'd Ibn Abu Waqqas, who is considered by the Chinese Muslims to be the first apostle of Islam to China. Abu Waqqas is reputed to have built China's first mosque in Canton and his purported tomb in the Islamic cemetery in Canton is now a Muslim shrine. The legend is clearly apocryphal but, as with all legends, does underline the early contacts between the Middle Kingdom and the Western Territories, as the Middle East was then known.

According to Tang annals, 651 is the formal date of the introduction of Islam to China. In that year they record that 'the King of Arabia sent for the first time an envoy with presents to the Chinese court and at the same time announced that the Arabs had already reigned 34 years and had had three kings'. The 'King of Arabia' was the third caliph, Uthman. It is interesting that in the same year as the official delegation from the Caliph Uthman to China in 651, the Persian Sasanid shah, Peroz, who ruled many of the areas later conquered by Islam, appealed to the Emperor, Kao Tsung, for support against the Muslim Arabs. Both China and the Sasanids saw a potential threat in the disruption of the Silk Road by the Islamic conquests and the former feared that the collapse of Sasanid Persia would strengthen the marauding Turkic tribes of Central Asia and encourage their attacks on China.

47   At Tongxin in Ningxia, a Hui man juggles his food over the frying pan with the skill of a master chef. In Islamic restaurants, recipes and ingredients conform strictly to Islamic dietary law.

48   (opposite) Kneading the heavy dough in preparation for making noodles, a kitchen helper at Xining performs the routine of stretching and rolling before threading the noodles by hand.

49   The famous Islamic restaurant in Canton.

Unlike his predecessor T'ai Tsung, who had declined requests for help against the Arabs, Kao Tsung encouraged and helped the Sasanids. As time went on, however, the flow of trade between the Middle East and China ensured a closer cultural understanding between these two peoples. The Tang annals referred to the Ta-shih (or Black Robed Muslims) and described them in the following terms: 'Ta-Shih comprises territory which formerly belonged to Persia. The men have large noses and black beards. They carry a silver knife on a silver girdle. They drink no wine and know no music. The women are white and veil their faces when they leave the house. There are great temples. Every seventh day the king addresses his subjects from a lofty throne in the temple in the following words: "Those who have died by the hand of the enemy will rise again to heaven; those who have defeated the enemy will be happy". Hence the Ta-shih are such valiant warriors. They pray five times a day to the Heavenly Spirit.'

Barriers between these two seemingly alien cultures did, however, exist and must have given rise to tensions. Chinese historical sources record one significant incident: 'In 713 an envoy appeared from Ta-shih bringing as presents beautiful horses and a magnificent girdle. When the envoy was presented to the Emperor Hsuan Tsung, he refused to "kowtow" (the customary obeisance) and said, "In my country we only bow to God and never to a prince." The Emperor at first wanted to kill the envoy but was persuaded by his ministers to tolerate the Ta-shih's culture and still not lose face!' Such cultural or political tensions did not, in the early part of the 8th century, lead to military confrontation between the Arabs and Chinese. However, according to Arab historical sources, Qutaiba Ibn Muslim, the Arab general, who had embarked in 705 on military campaigns in Central Asia, was meant to have crossed the Celestial Mountains into modern day Kashgar. The Chinese legends proceed to narrate that the Arab general

50   *Street food is popular outside the King Imin's Memorial Mosque where people gather for Friday prayer.*

had sworn to take possession of China but that a Chinese provincial governor had sent him a bag of Chinese soil to trample, a bag of coins as token tribute and a few young men as prisoners, thereby giving him symbolic possession of China and releasing him from his solemn oath to conquer the country.

The year 751, a century after Islam had officially first come to China, was an important milestone in Chinese Islamic history: it was the date of the Battle of Talas in which Chinese and Islamic forces crossed swords for the first time. The Arab armies defeated a Chinese army which, according to Arab sources, numbered 100,000, thereby paving the way for Islamic control of Central Asia. The capture of Chinese papermakers at the Battle of Talas introduced the manufacture of paper to the Islamic world and helped stimulate a flowering of culture and learning in the Abbasid capital, Baghdad.

During that era Arabia and China had within their respective empires at either end of the Silk Road two of the most powerful and populated cities in the world – Baghdad, or Madinat al-Salam (the City of Peace), and Ch'ang-an (the City of Eternal Peace), the imperial capital of the Tang Dynasty.

Ironically perhaps, just four years after the Arabs had defeated the Chinese at Talas, the foe became a friend when the Emperor Su Tsung appealed in 755 to 'A-p'uch'a-fo' (the second Abbasid caliph, Abu Ja'far al-Mansur) to help him recapture Ch'ang-an from An Lu-Shan, a military commander who had rebelled against the Tang Emperor and captured his capital city. The caliph sent 4,000 troops and the city was recaptured but his troops remained in China, intermarried with Chinese and formed a pioneering Muslim community in China – the forefathers, perhaps, of today's Chinese Muslim Huis.

53 Along the road from Turfan to Urumqi, an Uygur mother and child sit on the roadside selling grapes and dates.

54 (following pages) The harvest of grapes at the Turfan vineyard in Xinjiang Province.

51 (opposite top) Pepper, aubergine and tomato are favourites on vegetable stalls at Xining in Qinghai province.

52 (opposite bottom) At Putugou, where some of the best grapes are grown, two Uygur men hang bunches of grapes on vertical trellises for drying into raisins.

The earliest recorded Islamic sources for travellers' tales in China were entitled *Akhbar al-Sin wa-'l-Hind* or *Observations on China and India* and contain the records of the journeys and experiences of two Muslim travellers to China in the years 815 and 857. Abu Zaid came from Siraf, a town in the Arabian Gulf where goods from China were off-loaded and then transported in other vessels to Basra and Baghdad; he edited the story of a Muslim trader called Sulaiman who visited China in 851.

Sulaiman relates that at Kanfu 'which is the principal scale for merchants, there is a Muslim appointed Judge over those of his religion by the authority of the Emperor of China and that he is Judge of all the Muslims who resort to those parts. Upon several days he performs the public service with the Muslims and pronounces the sermon or *khutba* which he concludes in the usual form with a prayer for the Sultan of the Muslims. The Arab merchants who trade thither are in no way dissatisfied with his conduct or his administration in the post he is invested with, because his actions and the judgements

he gives are just and equitable and conformable to the Koran and according to Muslim jurisprudence.' The sea route from Arabia to China was hazardous and Sulaiman recalls the piracy, uncertain winds, frequent fires in Kanfu and extortionate port dues. Yet in spite of these hardships trade flourished.

Another Arab traveller was al-Mas'udi, the 10th century Arab historian whose *Meadows of Gold and Mines of Precious Gems* includes a detailed description of travels in China and the Arab trade enclaves that had sprung up in some of the coastal towns in China and in which the Arabs enjoyed a certain amount of extra-territorial privilege. The Muslim communities throughout Chinese history could not, however, isolate themselves from the vagaries of local politics and unrest and al-Mas'udi included in his works a detailed description of the Huang Ch'ao troubles, previously mentioned, in which some 120,000 foreigners, mostly Muslims, were killed.

55   At the door of the Ieytakar mosque in Kashgar, a fully veiled woman holds out a bunch of grapes for the Uygur men to spit on symbolically as they leave after their Friday service. The fruit is then considered to be blessed.

During the Tang Dynasty the Muslims who came and settled in China were for the most part mindful of the Golden Age of the Abbasids in which the Islamic Empire was as its most powerful. They were known as the Black Robed Muslims and were considered, and wished to be considered, as aliens. Their eventual integration as Chinese Muslims was a gradual process given impetus by the arrival of the Mongols and Genghis Khan, who destroyed the Abbasids in 1258 and the Sung Dynasty in 1260, and established the Yuan Dynasty.

During the Yuan Dynasty, Islam spread to the interior of China, forming communities in Gansu and Yunnan. Many Muslims were resettled from the Islamic lands which were under the rule of the Mongols and were given important posts in the civil administration and government bureaucracy. Kublai Khan appointed Shams al-Din Omar, known as Sayyid al-Ajall, who claimed descent from the Prophet Muhammad, as Governor of Yunnan in 1273. He was succeeded by his son and grandson and the tomb of Sayyid al-Ajall and his cenotaph in Canton are still today important testaments to this Muslim dynasty in Yunnan.

Marco Polo came across many Muslim enclaves on his travels in China during the Yuan Dynasty and the Arab traveller, Ibn Battuta, visited his Muslim brethren on his trip to China in 1324-1325: 'This [El Khansa or probably modern day Sian] is the largest city I have seen on the face of the earth. When we approached the city we were met by its judge, the presbyters of Islam and the great merchants. The Muslims are exceedingly numerous here. The whole city is surrounded by a wall, each of the six cities is surrounded by a wall. In the second division are the Jews, Christians and the Turks who worship the sun. There are in the city a great number of Muslims, with some of whom I resided for fifteen days.'

56 *Old Uygur men congregating for a traditional meal at Kashgar. With open palms, they offer the usual blessing before beginning to eat.*

57 *(following pages) A mural at the Bezeklik grottoes outside Turfan depicts a group of pilgrims from different ethnic backgrounds bearing tribute. Among them, to the upper right, is a man with a turban, indicative of people from the Middle East.*

58 (previous pages) The ancient ruined site of Subaxi outside of Kuqa
was once a monastic settlement along the Silk Road. The foreground is
a dried riverbed where the ancient city once spanned both banks.

59 A domed structure at Subaxi is all that remains of the altar of the
original temple.

61 *(following pages) The murals at Cave 17 of Kizil grottoes in Kuqa depict one of the Jataka stories about a previous life of the Buddha.*

60 *The grottoes at Kizil are set on an eroded hillside. Today access is restricted to a few wooden staircases connected to a scaffolding of balconies.*

The extensive foreign trade between the Middle East and China and the now vibrant Muslim communities in China introduced many technical and artistic skills which played an important role in Chinese history and development. Islamic techniques in astronomy resulted in improved methods of Chinese navigation and led to the founding in Beijing of the Royal Observatory by Jamal al-Din during the Yuan Dynasty. For several centuries after its foundation it was customary for a Muslim to be the Director of the Observatory.

In 1338 the Muslim calendar was adopted and was used for more than three centuries until it was replaced by the Gregorian calendar in 1669. According to Chinese sources, the influence of Muslim architectural designs can be seen in the work of the Muslim architect Ikhtiyar al-Din, whose design of the North Sea area of Beijing was claimed to be the precursor of the Imperial palace in Beijing. The Ming Dynasty saw the culmination of trade and cultural contacts between the Middle East and China. The Ming founder, T'ai-Tsuwas, was reputed to be a Muslim, but even if this cannot be verified, he was certainly greatly influenced by Islamic customs and was a devout man who forbade the drinking of wine and who encouraged the translation of many scientific texts into Chinese. Several naval expeditions from China to the Middle East were led by the Chinese Muslim admiral, Cheng Ho, more than one hundred years before the Europeans reached the Indian Ocean.

62   *The partial remains of a mural at Kumtula grottoes near Kuqa show the damage incurred by these historical sites along the Silk Road.*

63   *(following pages) The ruin of a signal beacon stands out against the mountains of Turfan along the Silk Road in Xinjiang.*

As a result of the increased flow of Chinese travellers into the Middle East, the great Ming geographies also contain detailed information on Arab cities such as Mecca and Medina. Chinese literature began to develop, influenced perhaps by the pilgrimage, the Hajj, which was for the first time undertaken by Chinese Muslims. In 1642 the first indigenous Chinese Muslim literature was created – the five volume *True Explanation of the Correct Religion* by Wang Tai-Yu. Another notable Chinese Muslim author and historian in the Ch'ing Dynasty was Liu Chih who had published several tomes on Islamic philosophy and law. In 1779 he published his most important work: the life of the Prophet Muhammad in twenty volumes.

The long history of Islam in China is a story of adaptation and compromise underlined by a fundamental inner cohesion which accounted for the survival of the religion in its Confucian environment. Throughout Chinese history the intermingling of these two religious systems, symbolically exemplified by the Chinese temple whose outward appearance belies its internal function as a mosque, was a delicate process. On many occasions it resulted in confrontation and bloodshed.

The 19th century saw several Muslim rebellions: in Yunnan, where Tu Hsui established a separate Muslim state for sixteen years and was known as Sultan Sulaiman; in Kansu where the leader, Ma Hualung, tried to establish an Islamic state; and in East Turkestan which was ruled for over fifty years by the Muslim, Yakub Beg. The 20th century saw the conflicts continuing, culminating perhaps in the repression and attempted abolition of religion during the Cultural Revolution and the flare-up of racial hostilities between various groups. Such lingering tensions were only recently rekindled by the publication of a defamatory book in Shanghai which offended the sensitivities of Muslims in China.

In spite of these conflicts and tensions, Islam is now viewed as indigenous to China. The religion which came with the Arabs over a thousand years ago is a living product fashioned from the interaction of China and Islam, perhaps echoing the words of the Emperor T'ai Tsung, the founder of the Tang Dynasty, whose reign saw the first formal contacts between these two great civilizations:

> Islam was once found only beyond the Western border. Who could have foretold that Muslims were to dwell in China forever?

64 Drawings of sheep or antelopes are found on the walls of Buddhist grottoes in Xinjiang.

PART 2

PERSONAL ENCOUNTERS

The initial indication that we were in a different China came the first day we were in Canton, the metropolitan city of southern China, fast undergoing economic change and modernization. It was early in the morning and the city was awakening to the bells of bicycles and horns of buses. We turned from the main street into an alley by the name of Dabizilu. This area was the Islamic quarter of Canton, where the first mosque in China was believed to have been built during the Tang Dynasty at the time of Sa'd Abu Waqqas.

66   (opposite) At a market in the streets of Akqi, two Uygur men modify their bicycles into devices which turn a grinding stone for sharpening knives.

65   An elderly Hui couple cycle into Tongxin for the Sunday market.

67 *Along the bank of the Yellow River at Zhongwei in Ningxia, a Hui engineer poses in front of his machine, a waterwheel which raises water from the river for irrigating fields nearby.*

From the outside, Wiaxinzu (Sage Memorial Temple) with its crimson walls had the same setting as many Chinese monasteries; beyond the walls, a different life was unveiled. Hajj Ma Fengda was waiting at the entrance. 'Salam 'alaykum.' His greetings ushered us into a whole different world – the realm of the Chinese Muslims.

Next to the entrance, an imposing white tower rising over 36 metres served as a minaret, but was once the guiding light for ships coming up the Pearl River, at the end of a hazardous journey from India, the Middle East,

or even further west. Ma told us with a chuckle that the pagoda leaning slightly to one side was interpreted by some as a deliberate motion of bowing to the west, the direction of Mecca.

In the courtyard were about twenty older women beginning their daily exercise of Tai Chi. In an adjacent courtyard, a few young men were performing a more rigorous exercise: 'Caquan', or Islamic boxing. Ma said that because of historic oppression, the Hui (Muslims of Chinese and Arab ancestry) had learned to defend themselves through the development of their own

68 *Inside a mud shed in Hotan along the southern Silk Road, an Uygur
man uses a cow to work a traditional mill.*

martial art. A story relates how the students asked the original teacher the name of this martial art. As the Islamic kung fu master was sipping his tea, he casually quipped, 'Caquan', meaning 'tea boxing'.

Hajj Ma, or *ahung* as the Chinese called the imam, went to Mecca with the Chinese Islamic Association in 1980 as an official group from the People's Republic of China. The group included fifteen other Muslims from all parts of China. Ma indicated that as today's individuals were getting richer because of economic reforms, more and more Muslims were making the

pilgrimage with their own funds. Indeed, we found out a month later that there were over 1,500 Muslims from Xinjiang alone who had been on the 1984 Mecca pilgrimage.

Wiaxinzu was closed by the government during the ten-year Cultural Revolution but was returned to the Muslims in 1982. Recently the mosque had received certain donations, but Hajj Ma assured us that the land held by the mosque produced enough rent to maintain the mosque and its related activities. Ma joined us for Friday prayers which started at 1.30 in the afternoon.

People began filing in around one o'clock. Some were Chinese in appearance except for the little caps they wore. Others had a Middle Eastern, darker complexion. They were of the Hui minority nationality. There were also Turkic-looking Uygurs from Xinjiang on China's western frontier who were doing business in Canton. Ma told us some surprising historical facts about the population. During the Tang Dynasty, there were only 50,000 indigenous inhabitants in Canton whereas the foreign population numbered over 100,000. Dabizilu, the name of the road where the mosque was situated, meant 'Great Benevolent Temple Road', a name with Confucian resonance. Closer examination revealed that it is actually a phonetic translation of 'Big Nose Road', a reference, Ma told me, to the features of

people from the Middle East. Even his family name 'Ma' was derived from the first sound of the name of the Prophet Muhammad.

During prayers, the men stayed to the front of the mosque while the women, in white veils, took up the last row. Afterwards, we retreated to a side chamber where Hajj Ma prayed for the family of a deceased Muslim. In the middle of the table, around which everybody sat, incense was burning in a censor.

It was symbolic that our first visit to a mosque was the Canton mosque, perhaps the first to be built in China. Our subsequent months were spent visiting six of the ten Muslim ethnic groups of China. The Hui, with a population of some 7.5 millions, and largest of the ten groups, was the first group we visited.

69   Along the bank of the Yellow River at Lanzhou, Luo Jungui and his family are the only household who still have traditional skin rafts; they are made from inflated sheep skins tied over a framework of willow branches.

Our train took us north towards Central China. At Chengzhou, a major railway junction, we were to change trains and travel westward. There are 60,000 Muslims and many mosques in Chengzhou, and some old Muslim settlements in the nearby city of Kaifeng, 70 kilometres away. Since we had a day's respite from travelling, we first visited the mosque on Liberation Road. The imam, Ahung Pan, or Abraham as he was also known, had come here from Ningxia. As a renowned scholar from a predominantly Muslim province, he had been offered a three-year contract to teach at this remote mosque. He served a community of 50,000 Muslims, and his contract would be extended if they liked his teaching.

Carrying an introduction from Ahung Pan, we took a taxi to Kaifeng. Jam Jenwen, 70 years old and one of the two ahungs at the Kaifeng East Mosque, was on hand to greet us. He told us there were six mosques in Kaifeng with over 30,000 Hui Muslims. His mosque served a community of 4,000 households and he used Arabic during its service. A stone tablet recorded the history of this Tang Dynasty mosque, with the first restoration in the year 1407 during the Ming Dynasty and a second one conducted in 1655 during the Qing. The most recent repair had been effected two years earlier.

A side building functioned as living quarters for older Muslim women who had no relatives. We observed Fatima, 80 years old, in a white veil performing her religious duties. Because she had a knee ailment, a long stool was provided for her; she could sit for prayer while bending her body in symbolic prostration. It was also interesting to see her using beads to count her prayers. A'isha, her friend, surprised us by reciting sections of the Koran in Arabic.

70 Uygur father and son team, near Kashgar, work together in forging a knife. The device next to the furnace is a blower for fanning the fires.

Our next train took us across China, passing Hanan, Shanxi, Shaanxi and Gansu into Qinghai Province. Here, with the help of Governor Hunag Jingpo, we acquired a jeep to take us thousands of kilometres into the field. Before departing on our expedition, we visited two mosques at Xining, provincial capital of Qinghai.

Friday prayers at the great mosque, as it was called, with over 5,000 devotees attending, was quite impressive. But we felt a lot more at home during our visit to a much smaller mosque – Yangjahang Mosque. It was late in the afternoon and many boys were there attending the evening school run by the mosque. In complete unison, they recited the Koran in Arabic. Behind the mosque were boarding rooms for some of the boys. One teenage boy proudly showed us a picture he had drawn of his beloved mosque.

A short walk from Yangjahang was the home of Ahung Ma Deming, or Shams al-Din. His hospitality was unmatched as we were poured rounds and rounds of tea. Dates and lump-sugar were added to produce more flavour. We were also offered biscuits and a variety of fried noodles. When it was Ma's teenage daughter's turn to pour our tea, we noticed the henna on her hand, evidence of the Islamic custom of dyeing one's fingers with the secretion of this plant. The plant was blossoming with little red flowers in their courtyard garden. Before we left, we were offered a rare hand-written copy of the Koran as a sign of friendship. We were pressed to accept this valuable gift and to avoid offending our host, eventually acquiesced, promising one day to present him with our book containing photographs of his family.

71   In the streets of Kashgar, an Uygur hat maker uses a sewing machine to produce caps.

Leaving Xining, we drove east for 150 kilometres to Lanzhou. Here by the bank of the Yellow River was a newly reconstructed mosque. They called their head teacher *imam* rather then *ahung*. Imam Yang Xin, or Yunis, had recently returned to his teaching post where he taught Arabic to young people as well as adults. Just a few years ago, he was condemned to hard labour during the Cultural Revolution. A highly educated man, his spirit was undiminished by seven years of banishment.

Yunis showed us his library of religious books which he had hidden during the Revolution and explained to us the difference between the 'New Sect' he believed in, and the 'Old Sect' of Islam. It seemed a paradox, but according to Yunis, the New Sect was seen as conforming to the traditional ways of Islam, and the Old Sect was a corrupted form. He gave some examples to clarify the matter for us. The old sect, he said, was incorporating Han culture and custom into its rituals, for instance, wearing black armbands when someone died, building memorial tombs for important people within the community, burning incense, or reciting the Koran when inviting guests for special occasions. According to Yunis, the New Sect was the purified form and interpreted the Koran in a more orthodox fashion.

While we were visiting this very picturesque mosque by the river, some children brought us freshly baked bread. People bring the flour to the bakery and pay a small fee for having their bread baked.

72 *A Kashgar bookseller has on his shelves several different versions of the Koran as well as other books in Arabic.*

A hundred or so metres down the road lived Luo Jungui, a Hui Muslim, who was the last of a disappearing breed in Lanzhou. Today Luo is the only individual in Lanzhou who is master of the art of making and operating a skin raft. These rafts, which were sometimes constructed from as many as 400 inflated sheepskins bound to a wooden frame, used to be floated all the way to Baotao in Inner Mongolia. Luo's raft consisted of fourteen sheepskins. We travelled on it a short distance down the Yellow River. Bridges spanning the Yellow River and motorized boats had made Luo's raft ferry obsolete, although it was again in demand owing to a

fresh influx of curious tourists. For a fee, he would demonstrate to them his skill with his raft.

From Lanzhou we drove north towards Ningxia, the smallest and one of the poorest provinces of China. Because the majority of the population were Hui, Ningxia was called a Hui Autonomous Region, like Xinjiang for the Uygur, Xizang for the Tibetans, Niumonggu for the Mongols and Guangxi for the Zhuang.

We saw few vehicles along the road as we entered some arid loess country. Along some stretches, the road had all but disappeared. Surprisingly at a roadside

73   At Yinchuan, capital of Ningxia Autonomous Region, a girl works a huge loom weaving a wool carpet with a traditional design.

petrol station, there was a long queue. We had a special supply of petrol coupons which were valid throughout the world. The attendants were concerned that some of us wore glasses. They were worried that long-sighted glasses would have the effect of a magnifying glass and were thus a potential fire hazard. This was a matter that was taken very seriously: a warning sign was posted outside the station forbidding anyone to enter with matches, glasses or even shoes with studs.

The road was getting worse by the kilometre as we bounced up and down in our seats. On one occasion, we asked for directions and were told to follow the asphalted road. Our problem was *finding* it!

At a ferry crossing near Zhongwei, we again came across skin-rafts. Here, in more remote reaches of the Yellow River, the rafts were still in regular use. We asked Karim how much he charged for each crossing. 'It costs ten fen (3 US cents) per crossing and ten more if wheeling a cart. But the fee rises and falls like the river. When the water rises, it is more dangerous, and more expensive. It is also more expensive for foreigners to cross.' We did not appreciate his humour!

74   A Kirgiz woman in the Pamirs weaving a long woollen belt to be used as a girdle for their family yurt

75   (following pages) A huge assortment of religious objects are offered by the Hui merchants to the Tibetans. Near Kumbum Gomba, south of Xinjiang, the trade is mainly controlled by the Hui.

Zhongwei was 400 kilometres from Lanzhou, and Yinchaun, the provincial capital, was another 200 kilometres away. For the last 100 kilometres, we finally found the black road. We were put up at a modern hotel and had an early meeting with Vice-President Wang Yenjen of the autonomous region. He promised that our request to meet with intellectuals and professional Muslims would be granted.

Dr Ma Chengyi was deputy-director and a urologist at the provincial hospital. He was working on a disease which affected a lot of Hui people, something he called 'Mediterranean anaemia'. We asked about dying and the Islamic belief in an afterlife. 'Hui people believe in an afterlife. When they die, they will go to heaven. After death, the body is cleansed, wrapped in white and a hole is dug in the ground for burial. The head to the north, the feet to the south, with the face turning west, towards Mecca.' 'You mean southwest,' We reminded him that we were now to the northeast of Mecca. 'But what about the Han?' We wanted to find out the difference. 'For Muslims who are going to die, they always want to go back to their homes and die there. But for the Han, they die in the hospitals,' answered Dr Ma.

76   Two Uygur jewellers of Kashgar crafting silver jewellery which includes rings, necklaces and earrings.

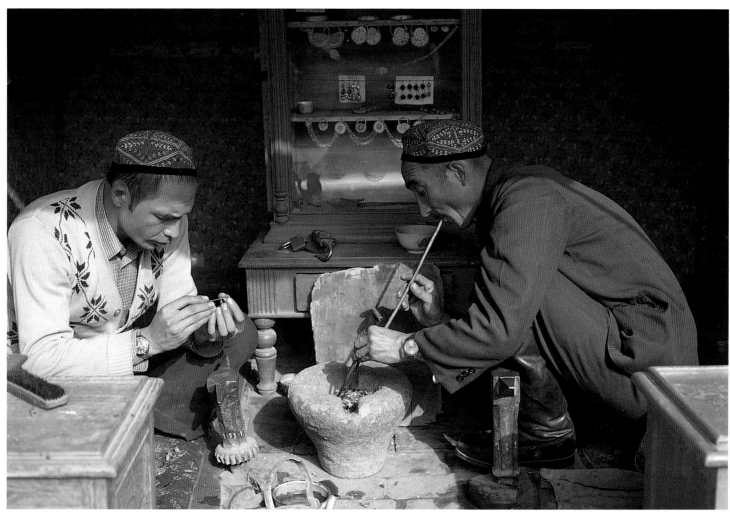

Many women patients prefer not to be examined by male doctors. We asked Dr Ma whether that was an attitude he had met. 'Not in the city. But in the countryside and the mountain region to the south, they are fundamentalists and even for an injection or inoculation, they would cut a hole in their clothes to get it. In emergency cases, the man has to tear up his own clothes and cover the woman up before they can do anything. You know, older women still wear a partial veil in the mountain region,' Ma explained.

We asked some people about birth control policies and how it was affecting the Muslims. Our questions were soon answered when one middle-aged man complained about the burden of having ten children.

At the university, we met Annie, a Hui professor of music. A nationally acclaimed singer in the 1960s, Annie described the use of the 'Kao-xuan' among Islamic women. It was a wind instrument made from bamboo, something like a mouth-organ in the shape of a comb and women wore it on their heads. 'Muslim women are forbidden to expose their hair to the sun and their faces to young men. So they always keep to themselves their feelings of happiness as well as sadness,' explained Annie. 'In the past, they were married off by the age of 13 or 14, so they used this instrument to voice their grievances.'

77   At the market of Kashgar, colourful saddles, bridles and other horse-related items are among the most sought-after merchandise.

78   (following pages) Along the fringes of the Taklimakan Desert in southern Xinjiang, horse and mule carts are common sights and widely used by the Uygurs for transportation.

79 (previous pages) A group
of cheering partygoers riding
an open truck along the road
between Kashgar and Yangisar
in southern Xinjiang.

80 Kirgiz girls with long
braided hair sit inside a yurt at
Sumutashi, west of Akqi by the
Soviet border.

At one meeting with intellectuals from the Islamic Association, a debate ensued on whether the Hui observed Ramadan and celebrated the Islamic New Year because of an ethnic lifestyle or a religious belief.

Before leaving Yinchaun, we visited an Islamic factory specializing in sweets and pastries. There were over 430 workers, mostly Muslims, producing 4,000 tons of pastry a year. The manager explained how the manufacture of Islamic mooncakes did not involve pig fat, unlike Han mooncakes. The Islamic Association came to the factory for a routine check, to make sure that the pastries were handled only by Muslim workers. Eventually they hoped the entire operation would be run by Muslims.

We travelled back to Lanzhou, then Xining, before heading south for Xunhua, up the Yellow River. Here against the beautiful setting of the Jishishan mountains live the 70,000 Salar Muslims. The hills have been eroded and the run-off of seasonal rain has made deep gullies in their sides. The Salars were harvesting their fields as we arrived. Men either wore a cap or a turban and women were veiled, the young with green veils, the middle-aged with black, and the old with white.

We were shown a large mosque which had just been completed. However, we were more interested in the historical Jeiji mosque. Jeiji was the oldest community when the Salar first moved to Xunhua some 700 years ago. The old men tell this story:

81 *Dressed in their best for the summer festivities, Kirgiz girls join in a game of tug-of-war, watched by a crowd at Sumutashi.*

In the past, there were two brothers from Samarkand by the name of Geleman [Gele meaning black and Man a name] and Ahman [Aha meaning white]. They were very religious people and well respected. Their popularity posed a threat to the local ruler who maliciously accused them of having stolen a cow. Though the two were vindicated, they decided to move away to avoid further confrontation.

With a Koran, eighteen followers, a white camel and some soil and water from their home village, the brothers left Samarkand and travelled east. In the course of their journey *a wāli* (a man learned in religion) explained to them the difficulty of their position. However, they passed on through Central Asia, Xinjiang, and reached southeastern Qinghai.

One evening, when they arrived in Xunhua, they lost their camel and so they camped at the present-day Jeiji village. In the morning they discovered the camel had already turned into a white rock. They compared the soil and water of this new place with that from their homeland and found that they were very much alike. So they settled and built their new home here.

Today a popular festival dance still depicts the Salars' long journey from Samarkand. Historical records showed that the Salar submitted to the rule of the Ming Dynasty in the year 1370. As a result, many historians consider this the date when the Salar settled in Xunhua. Their actual arrival was probably even earlier.

82   *Kirgiz women energetically involved in a game of tug-of-war with an audience of men wearing traditional white hats.*

The imam showed us their most sacred Koran, thirty volumes in all and bound in leather, and told us that they only managed to get it back from Beijing through the intercession of the Panchen Lama, head of the Chinese religious bureau, in 1983. 'But isn't the Panchen Lama the religious head of Tibetan Buddhism, not Islam?' we asked. He told us that the Salars' relationship with the Tibetans dated back many years, its origins remaining in local tradition.

After the Salar arrived in Xunhua, another forty-five followed from Samarkand, but they were all men and wanted to get married and have families. As all adjacent areas were inhabited by Tibetans, they tried to marry them. The Tibetans, being Buddhists, would not betroth their daughters to the Salars unless certain demands were met. The Salar were to put up images of Buddha, install prayer wheels on their roofs, hang prayer flags on poles in their courtyards, and put white rocks on the four corners of the roofs of their houses. Because of their Islamic beliefs, the Salar could not comply with the first three demands, but adopted the fourth. Today all Salar houses have white rocks decorating the corners of their roofs, similar to Tibetan houses.

The relationship between the Muslims and Tibetans was so close and longstanding that one Tibetan community at Kaligan to the south was converted to Islam about 200 years ago. This kind of conversion worked both ways. We were to find out later in Xinjiang that a group of Kirgiz in Yamin County were converted from Islam to Lamaism about 150 years ago.

83   Like the men, Young Kirgiz women participate in the tough game from which polo is derived.

We bade farewell to the Salar community and continued westward, travelling through the high grazing grounds of the Tibetans, the camel farms of the Mongols, and Gobi-like deserts, and arriving finally at Golmud some 800 kilometres away. The city is situated in the centre of the Qaidam Basin, at the end of the road south to Lhasa. From Golmud, we drove north for another 450 kilometres to reach the border with Gansu Province, at the Dangjinshan Pass. We saw our first yurt soon after we cleared the pass at 3,700 metres.

Here was a community of Kazaks. The term 'Kazak' means people with no master. The Kazaks of Aksay were not only a people without a master, but also a people without a home, at least since the 1930s. Most of China's one million Kazaks used to live in Xinjiang, but in 1934 and 1936 Kazaks from northern Xinjiang began a mass exodus that took them to Gansu, Qinghai and even Turkey.

Excessive oppression by the warlord, Xinxican, forced over 4,000 households with about 30,000 Kazaks to leave their traditional homeland in the Altai Mountains. Their intention was to move east to Gansu, thinking that the local warlord, Mabufeng, a fellow Muslim, would be sympathetic and accommodating. It turned out that Ma was just as brutal and employed Mongols and Tibetans to fight the Kazaks. Ma's troops systematically rounded up the Kazaks, disarmed them and decimated many families. The Kazaks were forced to move on again and many fierce battles ensued. Out of the 30,000 who had left Xinjiang, only about 5,000 remained in 1949. These ended up settling in remote regions of Qinghai and Gansu. The Aksay was one such group.

84　A Kirgiz hunter with his golden eagle preparing for flight.

85　(following pages) Kirgiz hunters of Sumutashi near Akqi with giant golden eagles perched on their arms ride out in groups as they begin their annual hunting season in October. Beyond the hills in the background is the Soviet Union.

We stopped our jeep near the yurts of the nomadic Kazaks. The barking of a huge mastiff brought out a few women. From a respectful distance, we explained the purpose of our visit. One young woman tightened the dog's leash on the wooden pole to which it was secured and which the animal had almost dragged out of the ground. She yelled at the dog while we proceeded cautiously inside the yurt.

A fire was burning in the central hearth. As soon as we sat down the women busied themselves preparing tea. A young girl, Khadija, aged about 20, spoke a local dialect, Putonghua. She turned out to be a school teacher from the nearby town of Aksay. There were eight children in the household, of which Khadija was the third. Names were taken from the Koran. When a new child was born, various names were called out while attempts were made to start a fire by striking a flint. The name which was called out just as the splint ignited the fire would then be adopted for the newborn.

We asked Khadija where her father was. He had gone to Beijing and on to Turkey to visit his relatives, she said. We asked how he could afford it. 'Life has prospered since the livestock were returned to the individual families after liberalization in 1979. Then after selling some of our sheep and the wool, he took the money with him and left,' answered Khadija. They still had over 500 sheep remaining. Every year, they sheared the sheep between May and June, yielding about 2,000 yuan (US$600), not a small income for a Chinese family.

We had heard of the famous Kazak songs and asked whether it was possible to hear some. Without embarrassment, the young teacher began singing some beautiful melodies. One was particularly moving: it told of a student going away to school with constant thoughts of his mother and was called 'Mother Love'. Later, the older women joined in and sang as well. To return their hospitality, we sang songs from Palestine and America.

A young boy brought out a two-stringed instrument, resembling a guitar, called a *dongbula*. We then heard a lengthy Kazak song called 'The Wild Horse with the Broken Leg' performed to the accompaniment of the *dongbula*. This traditional song is said to have been handed down from the time of Genghis Khan in the 13th century. It relates how the eldest son of Genghis Khan went hunting and shot a wild horse in the leg. While chasing the injured horse, he was murdered by an enemy. However, for a long time, nobody dared to break the tragic news to the Khan, dreading the anger of the fearsome Emperor. Genghis Khan sensed the disquiet among his entourage, and vowed to punish the bearer of any bad news by pouring molten lead into his mouth. While the situation dragged on, the Emperor became angry and his subjects suffered.

86 (opposite) While golden eagles are used by the Kirgiz for pursuing larger game, the hawk is used to catch small animals like rabbits and mouse hares.

87 (following pages) West of Mt. Muztagata in the Pamirs, Kirgiz use their yurts (felt tents) in the summer months as they migrate with their herds in search of grazing.

88   A Kirgiz family poses for a picture outside its yurt. The structure, similar to that used by Mongol, Kazak and Tajik, is collapsible and can be transported as the dwellers move in nomadic circuits.

A famous musician by the name of Haierbuke composed a song telling the unfortunate son's fate and played the song to Genghis Khan on the *dongbula*. Through its vivid portrayal of the galloping horse, the excitement of the hunt, and the eventual death of the son, the music conveyed the news to the saddened father. Genghiz Khan kept his vow: he poured the molten lead into the opening of the instrument.

In the evening, we were treated to a feast of a whole lamb, boiled in a huge pot. At dusk, the grandmother went out of the yurt, put a small rug on the ground, and began praying: these nomadic Kazaks had no mosque and prayed wherever they could. Their religion also exhibited some echoes of their shamanistic and animistic past since they still held sacred the sun, moon, water, fire, and other natural phenomena, though they considered themselves Muslims. That evening, we went to bed late after much music and song.

A hundred kilometres south of Aksay were the famous Buddhist grottoes of Dunhuang. We made a short pilgrimage there and proceeded north to Liuyuen, before turning west into Xinjiang. Nearby were the Jade Gate and the Sun Gate, two of the historic caravan posts of the Silk Road.

89 *The yurt is covered on the outside with felt and supported inside by a lattice framework of willow branches. In the summer, a lower portion of the felt can be turned upwards, as in this case, to allow ventilation. The Kazak family here live west of Golmud in Qinghai, and the man is holding a Kazak instrument similar to the Mongol* dongbula.

90 *(following pages) Two Kazak men west of Golmud lean against their yurt to stay in the shade on a hot afternoon. One of the men sits astride a wooden saddle on the ground.*

A road took us to Hami, 300 kilometres away. It was Shinghingsha, or Stars Gorge, which had the worst stretch of road. As there was a very good rail service between Gansu and Xinjiang, very few trucks travelled the Shinghingsha route. At Hami, we arrived in time to try the famous Hami melons, which were then in season, and later visited the great mosque as well as the 400-year old tomb of the Hami king. Here, the Uygurs, the six million Turkic-speaking people of Xinjiang, constituted the majority of the population.

The Turfan Basin was another 400 kilometres to the west. It is also called the Turfan Depression because it is one of the lowest parts of China, 154 metres below sea level. One of the driest areas in the world, here the summer sizzles at over 45°C. We were presented with a riddle: 'Why do people of Turfan wish the sun would shine brighter during the heat of the summer?' The answer from Xiao Zhang, our guide, came as a surprise. The basin was surrounded by snow-capped mountains, and the hotter the sun shone, the more snow would be melted to feed the underground channels for irrigation of farmland.

91 *A Kazak family from west of Golmud poses for a picture among tapestries with traditional Kazak designs.*

For hundreds of years, the Uygurs of this area have employed an irrigational system called the *karez*, a system with ancient origins in the Middle East. The *karez* are underground channels which water about five percent of the farmland in Xinjiang. In the country around Turfan, there are over 1,300 of these underground channels, varying in length from 3 kilometres to 14 kilometres.

Wells are sunk at 10 to 30 metre intervals, beginning in the foothills of the mountains, where water can be found underground. A long series of these shafts are used to facilitate the tunnelling of horizontal underground channels which help direct the water towards human settlements for irrigation and drinking purposes. The wells in the foothills can be as deep as 80 metres; but as the land descends from the foothills they become shallower. The horizontal underground channels get closer to the surface as they run away from the foothills, until eventually they became a surface stream. The wells require maintenance every year or so. Each channel may be used for 150 to 300 years before eventually drying up.

We were taken to Putugou, or the Valley of Grapes, where some of the best grapes of China are grown. The Uygurs were harvesting the grapes. The seedless ones were carted away for making raisins. Inside some mud-brick houses with holes in the walls, men were hanging up bundles of grapes on vertical trellises. These trellises reach from the floor to the ceiling and on each are hung approximately 100 kilos of grapes. The natural drying takes about a month and each 100 kilos yields 20 kilos of raisins, retaining 60 percent of the sugar content. We tried some raisins. They were seedless, but many had small pieces of stems attached to them.

While we were sitting in a vineyard tasting the different varieties of grapes, we overheard a debate by two Uygur cadres. They were arguing over whether grapes were better in the Soviet Union or in China. One cadre insisted that those he had tried in the USSR in the 1960s were sweeter than those here. The other disagreed. Finally a third cadre arbitrated and said, 'Of course those in the Soviet Union were better. In the 1960s, we sent all our best grapes to them.' Everybody laughed in agreement. We left Turfan thinking that the Russians probably had the best Hami melons as well.

Some five hundred kilometres southwest of Turfan was Kuqa, an ancient city along the Silk Road. Today there are still old ruins near the city. Subashi is one of

these sites. Liang Heicheng, Director of the Cultural Relics Department, was our host. As we drove out of town and up a nearby hill, the outline of a fairly large city could be seen in the far distance and we strained to hear the hum of city life carried by the wind. As we got closer, we saw that the city was actually astride two banks of a dried river and was about two kilometres wide. Most of the city had already been eroded by the desert winds and all that remained were merely the skeletons of buildings and structures. As we walked through streets and alleys, we seemed to hear whispers of ghosts telling tales of the Silk Road's past.

He Ling, our driver, discovered an ancient coin sticking out of a wall. He took it out and showed it to us, but Mr Liang, the Director, already had his hands out and we handed it over.

92 A Kirgiz mother and daughter sewing and doing needlework near Akqi in western Xinjiang.

93 (following pages) Needlework design on tapestry of the Pamir Kirgiz.

94 (opposite) Traditional design adorns a felt rug used as a door for a Kirgiz yurt on the Pamirs.

95 (following pages) Silver rings worn by Kirgiz women living at Sumutashi west of Akqi, near the Soviet border with China.

He said the sweeping wind continuously eroded the surface of the site and occasionally old coins and other relics were uncovered. However, everything found belonged to the state and had to be given up.

We visited two exceptional Buddhist grottoes, Kizil and Kumutula. Kizil had 236 caves and almost 10,000 square metres of murals. The murals were exquisite and we were given the rare opportunity to photograph some of them. Many depicted Buddhist stories as well as the history of the trade route. After the incident at Subashi, He Ling, our driver, was no longer interested in any treasure trove.

We went on to Aksu, and westward towards the border region with the Soviet Union. At the country town of Akqi, we visited the Kirgiz. Of the 120,000 Kirgiz in China, many live near the frontier. We drove westward for another fifty kilometres and arrived at Sumutashi, a small Kirgiz community a short distance away from the border. We were told the Russians were just over the hills. There were thirteen points where the national borders were in dispute in Xinjiang. One of these was here at Sumutashi. Many people had experienced difficulties while herding sheep in the border region.

Every year the Kirgiz, who are nomads during the summer but in winter live in permanent homes, congregate in their traditional summer pasture in the disputed area. Nomads from both sides of the border traditionally grazed their animals there peacefully. Indeed, some of the nomads were related though they were from different sides of the present border. However, the new status quo between the two powerful nations has changed all that. Today the Chinese Kirgiz continue to use the summer pasture, but from the Russian side come only the border military patrols. This has made the situation very tense at times. Abdullah, a shepherd, was once captured by the Russians and detained for three days before being released. Perhaps one day the cross-border difficulties will ease and the Kirghiz will once again be able to travel back and forth to visit their friends and relatives.

From mid-October and throughout the winter months, many Kirgiz men are involved in a unique sport – hunting with giant eagles. They go out in groups or individually, taking with them their treasured birds of prey. These expeditions are taken very seriously. In fact, for the experienced eagle-hunters, it has become a very lucrative business, and an important part of their economy. Of about 1,000 households in Akqi, over 150 have golden eagles. We talked to Kumashi, a thirty-seven year-old Kirgiz, who was a famous eagle-hunter.

Close to his home he kept his eagle, called Bosom, meaning 'two-year-old', because that was its age when caught. At five years old, Bosom had a wing-span of about seven feet. Reaching its prime between the age of four and eight and living to twenty, Kumashi said Bosom could easily fetch 300 to 400 yuan if sold. But he had no intention of selling his pet because, in the last season alone, it had netted him over 200 yuan with its prey. Bosom had caught eight rabbits and eight foxes in the previous year. As each fox skin fetched about 25 yuan, it produced a good income for Kumashi's family. This year they would be hunting the yellow goat instead. The Kirghiz practised an ecologically sound policy of annual rotation of prey allowing the animals in the wild to maintain their population level.

We talked at great length about the three different methods of capturing the eagles, and how each method and the age at which they were caught affected the temperament of the bird. For example, those caught as baby birds from a nest in the wild would grow up to be more noisy and spoilt because they were not afraid of people. Kumashi also explained the method used in training an eagle: how they are fed, then starved, bathed with hot water, made to stand on strings and not allowed to sleep until finally they are tamed. This sets the stage for the next process of training which includes tying the tail feathers with strings, releasing the bird with a long leash, and giving it a carefully controlled diet.

We went on a short expedition to learn how the eagles hunted, but it was not the right season and we came back with no prey. Riding out with these giant birds perched on our arms was an interesting balancing act for novices like us. Whenever an eagle lost its balance, it flapped its wings to stabilise itself while maintaining a much firmer grip on the rider's arm. It was not easy to keep both the eagles and ourselves balanced on horseback, and we came back with our arms marked and bruised in spite of the thick gloves we had been wearing.

96　(opposite top) Kazak design on bags used by the people at Aksay in northwestern Gansu.

97　(opposite bottom) This screen is made of willow twigs and brocaded with coloured woollen threads. It is used by the Kirgiz of the Pamirs inside the yurt to partition the kitchen and storage area from the main living quarters.

98　(top) Silver fasteners adorn this Kirgiz woman's jacket.

99　(bottom) Silver ornaments with traditional designs worn next to the waist adorn the Kirgiz woman's costume.

102 Guests at a wedding in the Pamirs.

100 (opposite top) Knives made at Yingisar along the southern Silk Road are renowned among the Uygurs. These decorative examples with six inch blades show Middle Eastern influence.

101 (opposite bottom) A necklace with coral, beads and stones is among the dowry of a newly-wed Tajik bride of the Chinese Pamirs.

103 (following pages) A Tajik wedding in the Pamirs is a three day festival. On the second day before the bride leaves her maternal home, much of the celebration of dancing, singing and feasting centres around the hearth and large adjacent area. The bride, standing, wears a white veil covering her face, a red scarf and strings of buttons braided to her long hair.

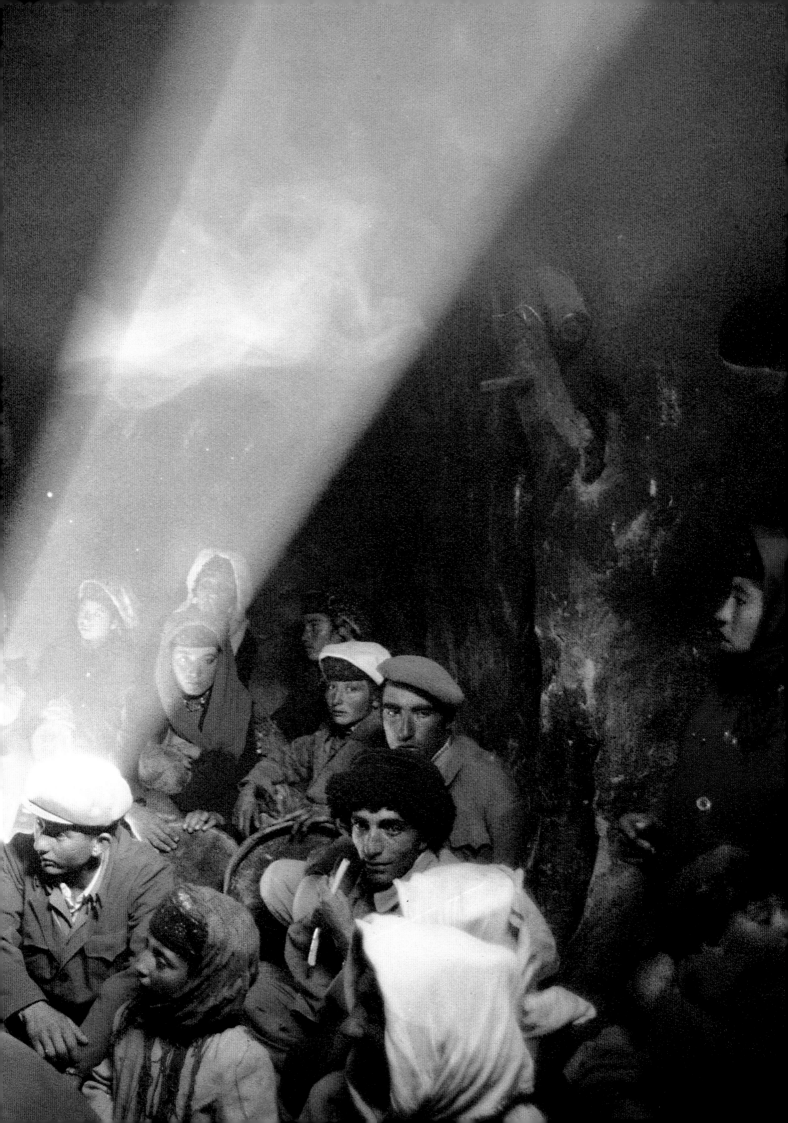

104 (previous pages) The Tajik groom wears a turban of twisted red and white scarves. Over his shoulders is sprinkled white flour, symbolic of good luck for his marriage.

105 (previous pages) As friends and relatives gather at the bride's home, there is dancing and feasting about the hearth all night long. Two men with flutes made from eagle bones play to the accompaniment of drums beaten by the women.

106 (previous pages) As the wedding party moves outside the house during the day, there is more dancing. Graceful Tajik dances recall the outspread wings of eagles in flight.

107 (previous pages) Colourfully dressed in silk shirts, boots and embroidered hats, a group of young Tajik mothers look on with their children as the wedding party proceeds. Buttons attached to their braids signify their marital status.

108 (previous pages) On important occasions Tajik women of high status wear jewellery to adorn themselves. The silver headdress is usually worn by the bride or the newlywed.

109 (previous pages) An old Tajik plays an eagle bone flute at the wedding party in the Pamirs.

110 (previous pages) Tajik horsemen in the Pamirs conduct a violent game of primitive polo.

After our experience with the birds, we settled in a Kirgiz yurt for tea and yoghurt. Our host brought out a musical instrument called a *komuz*, a small, unfretted type of three-stringed lute. Practically everyone learns to play it from childhood. As the Kirgiz saying goes, 'You are born to the sound of the *komuz*, you live your life to its melodies, and it accompanies you to your grave.' It was used for some impromptu songs, lullabies, wedding songs, melodies for bidding guests farewell, herding songs and the national epic called *Manas*. This tells of how the Kirgiz nation was formed and unified, and of life and social conditions in the Middle Ages. After explaining the general theme of the song, our host began singing this famous *Manas*. Since it is divided into eight parts and is over 200,000 lines long, we were satisfied with some sample verses.

We continued our journey southward, skirting the Taklimakan Desert. Kashgar, or today's Kashi, was at a major crossroads on the old Silk Road. Today it remains one of the largest centres of Central Asia. Its Sunday bazaar is still perhaps the largest in existence, with over

111 A camel cart with huge wooden wheels passes along the edge of the Taklimakan Desert in southern Xinjiang.

50,000 people attending. A huge variety of stalls and vendors were divided into different sections. Those selling clothes, fabric and hats were in one section. Others displayed carpets, bags, and boots. Still others were selling pottery and porcelain wares, leather, furniture, knives, jewellery and other metal utensils. A couple of stalls were offering new and old books and curios such as silver coins and ornaments. The food section had everything from seasonal and dried fruits, vegetables, and other consumables to daily necessities like flour and sugar.

One impressive sight in Kashgar was the large mosque in Iteger Square. On Fridays it housed six to seven thousand Uygur devotees. We joined the prayers and the atmosphere was reminiscent of the Middle Ages. People were dressed in various ways, they looked different, and had caps or turbans. When the prayers came to an end, we filed out through the door. A few women, some of them in full brown veils, lined the doorway. They were holding either plates of grapes or teapots. As the men left the mosque, they spat at the fruits or the containers. Some did so symbolically. Others actually spat. We asked the meaning of this custom and were told that the now-sacred grapes and teapots would be taken home to help cure the sick. We hoped the remedy would come by looking at, rather than eating, the grapes, or drinking from the pot.

Our team travelled onward along the southern Silk Road to Hotan where our interest turned to the modern silk industry. 'Modern' proved, however, to be the wrong word, as we soon discovered when we investigated production beyond the new silk factory in the city. For here, in the countryside, there were Uygurs still engaging in the time-honoured tradition of growing mulberry trees, raising silkworms, reeling the silk from cocoons on traditional wooden wheels, spinning the silk, dyeing it, and finally weaving the silk fabric on wooden looms, exactly as their forefathers had done for centuries. This will remain for us one of the most sensational and evocative images of the Old Silk Road.

112   A Tajik baby girl riding with her mother through the Pamirs. The Tajiks are a Persian speaking group in China numbering 26,000.

As a by-product of the silk industry, paper was still hand-made by one family, piece by piece, from mulberry bark. As we watched the wooden frames which held one paper at a time for drying, we realized we might be seeing the last of a dying craft. Nearby, a papermill's machines were turning out paper by the roll.

We next proceeded to Yutian before turning back towards the Pamirs – the Roof of the World. Near Kongur and Muztagata, two mountains over 7,500 metres, we visited other Kirgiz nomads. But our main goal here was to see the Tajik, the only Shi'ite Muslims of China and 26,000 in number.

Taxkorgan was the seat of government of the Tajik Autonomous Region. Historically, the northern and southern route of the Silk Road joined here before leaving China. In Chinese history the Pamirs were called 'Zongling', meaning Onion Range. The name is possibly accounted for by the many wild onions which grow around the mountains. The town of Taxkorgan was called Shitoucheng, or Stone City. As the journey over the stony roads had left the jeep with many flat tyres, the name of the city seemed very apt. Legend has it that a Chinese princess was betrothed to a man in the West but ended up settling here because of an unexplained pregnancy. Today only the ruins of an old fort called Princess Fort remain to verify the story.

113   A Tajik boy near the Afghan border drinking yoghurt from a bowl. He wears the male's traditional lambskin hat.

114   (opposite) A Kirgiz boy with a traditional black and white woollen hat plays with his pet cat near Mt. Muztagata in the Pamirs.

115 (previous pages) An Uygur mother and child from Yutian, east of Hotan, along the southern Silk Road. Here the women wear a traditional little cap over their veils made of wool at the bottom and silk on the top.

116 (opposite) An Uygur boy with an embroidered cap near Turfan on the Silk Road.

117 (top) At an elementary school at Sumutashi west of Akqi by the Soviet border, Kirgiz children learn to write in Chinese as well as their native tongue.

118 (following pages) Two Uygur girls outside the mosque of Kuqa.

119 (following pages) A Kirgiz student at Sumutashi west of Akqi works out some mathematical problems in the presence of the teacher.

120 (following pages) The King Imin Memorial Mosque outside Turfan is well attended by the whole community every Friday.

At Taxkorgan, we saw the first group of Uygurs returning from the pilgrimage to Mecca. They were loaded with the merchandise they had brought back. Outside the hotel, a few were busy peddling some of the items. One man was complaining about the heavy duty levied on his luggage by the Chinese Customs. His companion consoled him by reminding him that he had just acquired the title of Hajj, an honour given only to someone who had made the pilgrimage.

Sadly, it was not possible for us to continue along the Silk Road. At that time talks had only just begun to open up the Pamirs road between China and Pakistan, to provide a port of entry for foreigners as well as Chinese and Pakistani nationals. Such negotiations take a long time and the two sides were still exchanging protocols. In fact, while we were in Taxkorgan, the border customs officials from Pakistan arrived for their first visit.

121   (previous pages) While girls and boys are not allowed into the main portal of the mosque at Turfan, they can observe prayers from a balcony on the second floor. From the windows they can look out onto the market.

123   (opposite) A boy at the boarding school of Yangjiaxiang mosque in Xining proudly displays a picture he has drawn of his favourite mosque.

124   (page 144) A red wall poster with Chinese characters is stuck to the wall of a mosque at Yinchuan in the Ningxia Hui Autonomous Region. Rather than the usual political slogan common on such posters, the text reads: 'Propagate the fine traditions of the Islamic religion.'

Instead, we explored some side 'roads' and took a long-overdue bath at a nearby hotspring before joining a jubilant wedding party of Tajiks at a remote village. The three-day festivities left us exhausted. We ate and drank, joined in the celebrations and finally followed the bride and groom to their new home. While participating in these celebrations in China's farthest outpost, we happened to listen to a broadcast from Beijing. The Chinese capital was also celebrating a national holiday. It was 1 October, 1984. At times it seemed difficult to believe that the Pamirs and Beijing were part of the same country. What struck us at that moment with such intensity was that Islam, a movement which had started in Arabia fifteen centuries ago, could still be the binding force among such distant and disparate peoples.

122   At the great mosque of Xining, a young Hui boy poses for a picture as others perform their ablutions for the Friday prayer. Children are taught at an early age about Islamic religious observances.

PRINCIPAL EVENTS AND DYNASTIES IN CHINA AND ISLAM

618-907 Tang Dynasty 622

The Hijra of Muhammad from Mecca to Medina
and the beginning of the Muslim era
632-661 the Orthodox Caliphs First contacts with
China

661-750 the Umayyad Caliphate

751 the Battle of Talas

749 the 'Abbasid Caliphate

907-960 Five Dynasties
and Ten Dynasties

960-1279 Sung Dynasty
1215 Genghiz Khan seizes Beijing
1279-1368 Yuan Dynasty

1258 Mongols sack Baghdad
1206-1634 Mongol Great Khans

1281-1924 The Ottomans

1368-1644 Ming Dynasty
1644-1912 Ching Dynasty

1501-1732 Safavids in Persia
1526-1858 Great Mughals in India

1949 establishment of the
People's Republic of China